the MENTAL LOAD

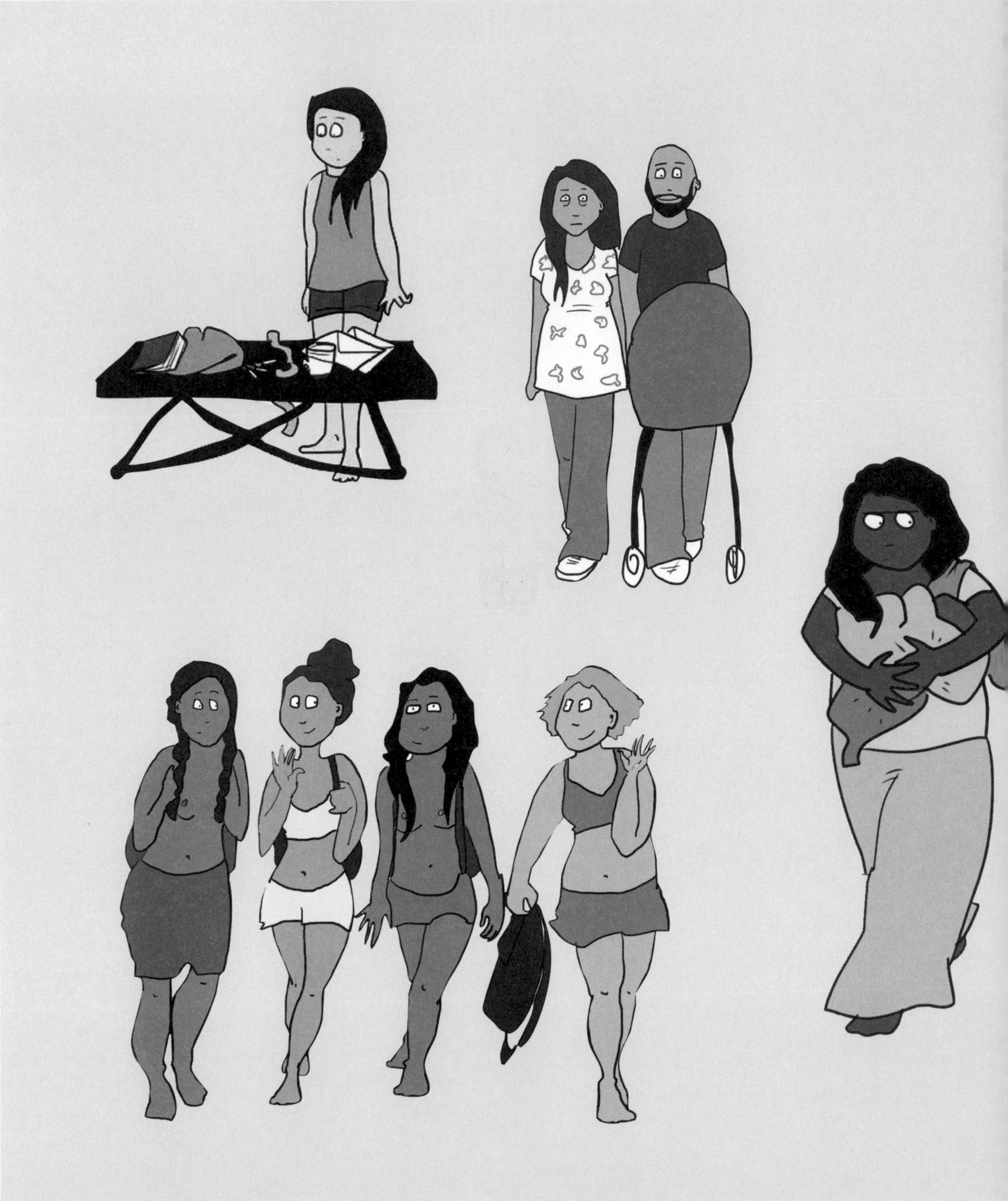

the
MENTAL
LOAD
A FEMINIST COMIC

EMMA

TRANSLATED BY
UNA DIMITRIJEVIC

SEVEN STORIES PRESS
NEW YORK • OAKLAND • LONDON

SEVEN STORIES PRESS
140 Watts Street
New York, NY 10013
www.sevenstories.com

College professors and high school and middle school teachers may order free
examination copies of Seven Stories Press titles. To order, visit www.sevenstories.com or
send a fax on school letterhead to (212) 226-1411.

Book design by Carlotta Colarieti and Abigail Miller

ISBN 978-1-60980-918-8 (pbk)
ISBN 978-1-60980-919-5 (ebook)

Printed in China

9 8 7 6 5 4 3 2 1

TABLE *of* CONTENTS

INTRODUCTION
vii

1
You Should've Asked
3

2
Violence of the Oppressed
23

3
The Story of My Friend C.
33

4
The Male Gaze
43

5
Show Me That Bosom
55

6

The Wonderful Tale of Mohamed

71

7

The Wait

83

8

Work!

103

9

Check Your Pussy!

131

10

Just Another Guy from the Hood

145

11

Chill Out

159

12

The Holidays

185

INTRODUCTION

UNTILL 2010, I was a little model citizen. I studied, and then I worked. I gave to charity, I voted, and I recycled.

I could see that things weren't going well in the world, and I thought that it was because of people who didn't study, didn't work, didn't give to charity, didn't vote, and didn't recycle.

Aged 30, I partly found myself on the side of those who bear the brunt of the system.

I realized that far from contributing to the improvement of my society, I had participated in its downfall. I had a political awakening.

I quickly understood that on my own, I couldn't shake things up. In order to act, we must be many.

That's the power of collective intelligence: if we all influence the decisions that concern us, only then will they be made in the general interest.

But if we continue to rely on a handful of leaders, they will serve their own.

It's hard to escape our social conditioning, and the more I spoke to people, the more I was confronted with my own preconceptions. We couldn't stand up for ourselves, the world was the way it was, we had to do as we were told, and not complain: study, work, vote, recycle, and teach the same things to our children.

So I began to draw my ideas. Maybe by turning them into images, I could help others rip the veil from their eyes and experience their own political awakening, as I had been lucky enough to do.

It worked. We were 30, then 1,000, 40,000, and today 200,000 to collectively discuss the concept of a fairer world, one in which the dignity of each person would be preserved.

Collective intelligence has no borders, and I know that all around the world, many citizens are already getting involved and discussing this future society.

My stories are a tool that I want them to make use of.

It's for this reason that they've been translated for you, English-speaking citizens of the world.

I hope that these pages will find their place in your grassroots struggles, just as they have in France.

What follows is two years of social analysis and observation in pictures, which I hope will also resonate with you.

the MENTAL LOAD

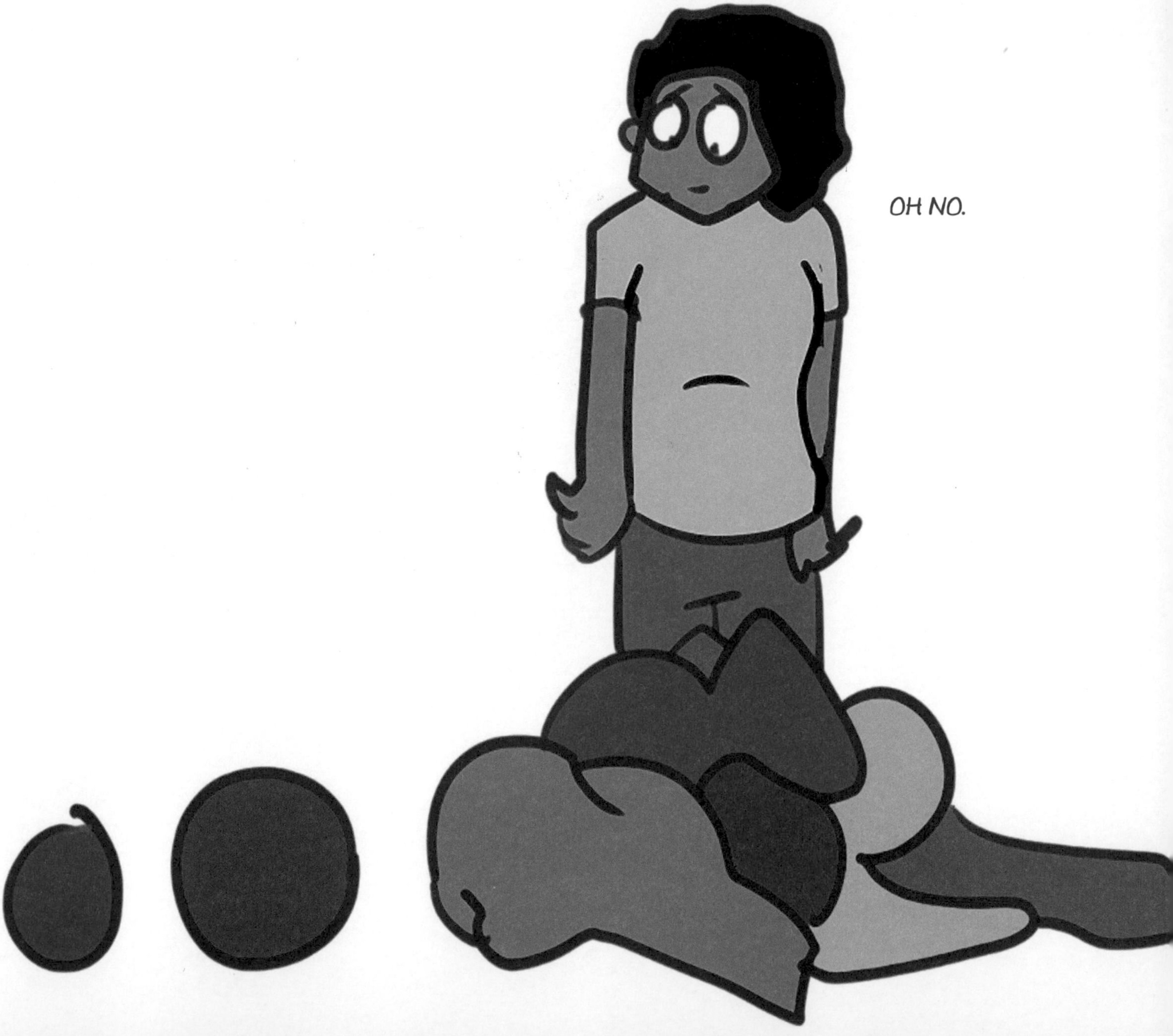
OH NO.

1
You Should've Asked

Back when I was in my first job, a colleague invited me over for dinner.

When I got there, she was trying to feed her kids while preparing our meal.

After a while, the pot started
to overflow . . .

Come on
sweetie, make
an effort.

. . . and everything spilled
onto the floor.

OH NO!

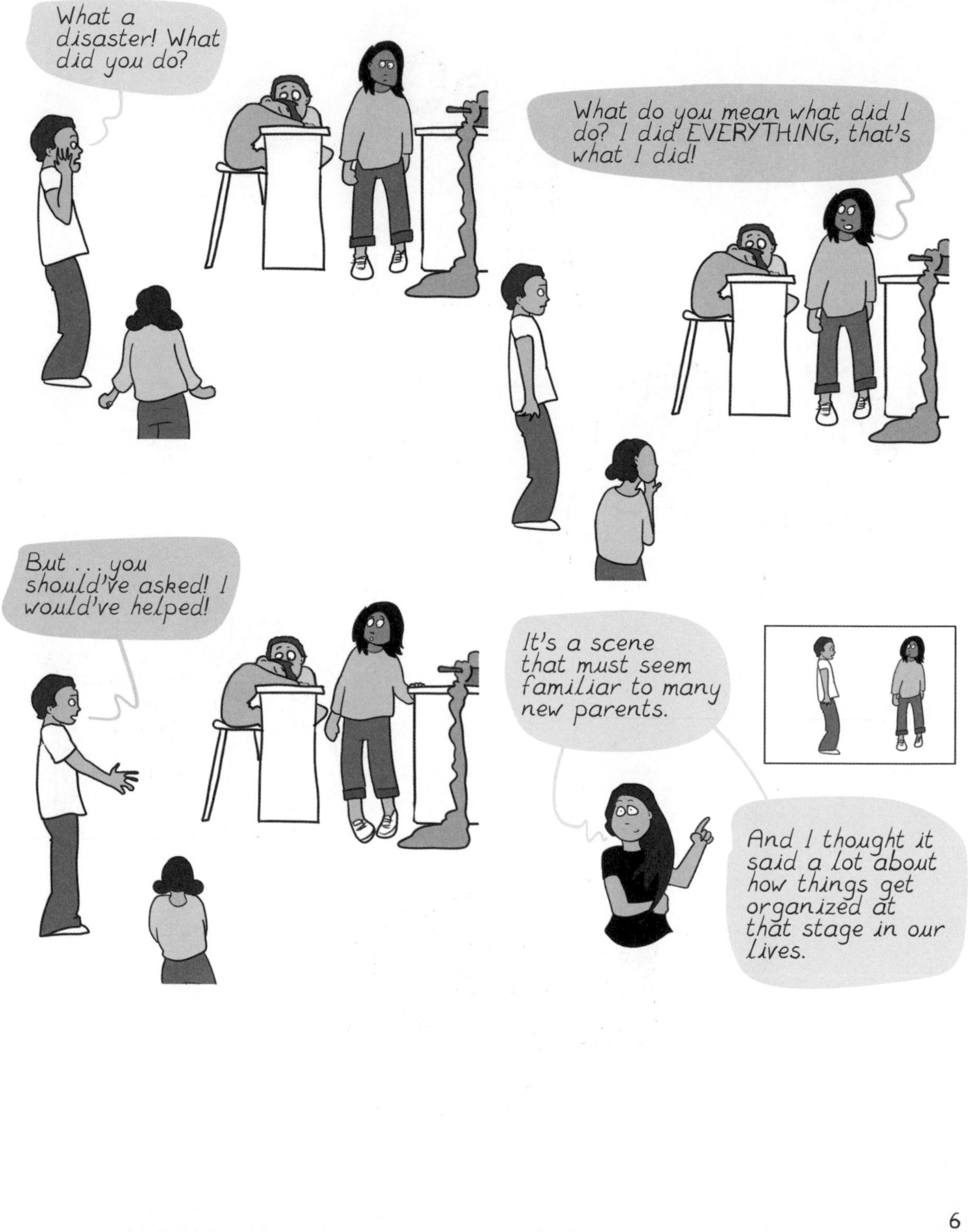

What a disaster! What did you do?
What do you mean what did I do? I did EVERYTHING, that's what I did!
But . . . you should've asked! I would've helped!
It's a scene that must seem familiar to many new parents.
And I thought it said a lot about how things get organized at that stage in our lives.

When a man expects his partner to **ask him to do things**, he's viewing her as the manager of household chores.

"Household management"
Project Leader

Underling

So it's up to her to know what needs to be done and when. The problem with that is that planning and organizing things is **already** a full-time job.

So, delivery in a month, let the developers know, ask the client about bullet point 10 in the file . . . oh crap, it's 7 p.m!

At work, once I started managing projects, I quickly stopped participating in them. I didn't have the time.

So when we ask women to take on this task of organization, and at the same time to execute a large portion, in the end it represents 75% of the work.

Feminists call this work **the mental load**.

The mental load means always having to remember.

Remember that you have to add cotton swabs to the shopping list.

Remember that today's the deadline to order your vegetable delivery for the week.

Remember that we should have paid the caretaker for last month's work by now.

That he needs to
get his booster
shot.

That the baby grew
another 3cm and
can't fit into his
pants anymore.

Or that your part-
ner doesn't have a
clean shirt left.

The mental load is almost completely born by women.

It's permanent and exhausting work. And it's *invisible*.

So while most heterosexual men I know say that they do their fair share of household chores, their partners have a rather different perspective.

For me, the fact that this load exists becomes obvious when I decide to take care of a simple chore, like clearing the table.

I start by picking something
up to put it away,

but on the way I come
across a dirty towel that
I go put in the laundry
basket,

OH

which I find full.

So I go to the washing
machine,

... and I see the vegetables that I need
to put in the fridge.

As I'm putting away the vegetables,
I realize that I need to add mustard
to the shopping list.

And so on and so forth.
In the end, I'll have cleared away my table after 2 long hours.

Only to find it covered in stuff again later that evening.

If I ask my partner to clear the table, he'll just clear the table.

OH NO!

The towel will stay on the floor,

the vegetables will rot on the kitchen counter,

OH NO . . .

OH NO.

and we won't have any more mustard for dinner.

It's like when my friend J., on her way to bed, asked her husband:

Can you take the baby's bottle out of the dishwasher when it's done?

. . . and getting up for the first nightly feed found the dishwasher open, with just the bottle on the counter, and everything else still inside.

OH NO.

Waaaaaa

What our partners are really saying, when they ask us to tell them what needs to be done, is that they **refuse to take on their share of the mental load.**

Let me know if you need help.

Of course, there's nothing genetic or innate about this behavior.

We're not born with an all-consuming passion for clearing tables,

just like boys aren't born with an utter disinterest for things lying around.

But we're born into a society,

in which very early on we're given dolls and miniature vacuum cleaners,

Look at that dainty little boy with his little tea set!

and in which it seems shameful for boys to like those same toys.

In which we see our mothers in charge of household management, while our fathers only execute the instructions.

And in which culture and media essentially portray women as mothers and wives, while men are heroes who go on fascinating adventures away from home.

This conditioning will take effect from our earliest years, and on into adulthood.

And while women are more and more present in the workforce, they still remain the only ones in charge of the household.

When we become mothers, this double responsibility blows up in our face.

11 days after we go through the ordeal of giving birth, our partner goes back to work.

Goodbye, my love . . .

Off to save capitalism

And it seems normal to him.

During this time, while recovering from our stitches in between two sleepless nights, we'll be thinking about everything that concerns the baby.

Choosing a nanny . . .

. . . buying clothes . . .

. . . medical check-ups . . .

. . . preparing meals.

And once we're back at work, things will get so hellish that it will feel less exhausting to keep doing everything than to battle with our partner so that he does his share.

I'll stop by the supermarket.

That's why you find fathers with children who are already a few years old who still don't know where to buy their clothes, what to feed them, when they need their next vaccination, or even what the nanny's phone number is.

Of course, there's nothing forcing us to do all this.
The problem is that when we stop, the whole family suffers.

So most of us feel resigned to the fact that we are alone in bearing the mental load, nibbling away at our work or leisure time just so we can manage everything.

So. I already know what some people are gonna say:

It's not true, I take care of half the chores at home.

In that case, just as well! (But try and confirm it with your partner.)

If things are like that in your home, it still doesn't change the problem: statistically, women are still the ones managing household tasks.

According to the French Institute of Statistics, women are still devoting 2.5 times more hours to chores than men.

And if this gap has been narrowing, it's not because men are doing more . . .

. . . but because wealthier households outsource these tasks, most often to poor immigrant women.

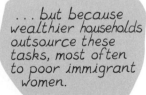

We can't really say that it's a good solution.

No, for things to change, it seems clear that men have to learn to feel that their home is also their responsibility.

For a start, it would be good if fathers insisted on their right to be with their family in the first months of their child's life.

Right now, only feminists are demanding longer paternity leave, and without much success. It's time to take the lead!

It can also help to start from the beginning, and to divide up recurrent and non-critical chores,

even if that means becoming a bit more tolerant of stuff lying around!

And also, sometimes simply leaving the house without preparing everything beforehand, and not feeling guilty about it!

A role reversal can often be more effective than confrontation.

And of course, raising our children as far away as possible from stereotypes,

to offer them a fairer future than the one we've got!

But even with all that, we've got to admit that it's complicated to manage a household when both parents work full-time.

I think it's important to ask ourselves why we have so little free time to do all that.

Is there really no other option but to spend so little time at home and so much time at work?

I think that's up for debate!

2
Violence of the Oppressed

It's February 2016 and the French government has decided to dismantle the Labor Code.

Most French citizens are against the project.

So we're out demonstrating.

We face the full brunt of police violence.

Protesters organize themselves into an improvised medical service to give first aid to the wounded.

Yet on the news, nobody mentions it. All they talk about are the "hooligans," these protesters who are smashing billboards and throwing eggs at the riot police. It makes me think of the suffragettes' protests, and how back then, those standing up for their rights were only met with violence.

Six years ago, I found myself working in a very male-dominated office.

To make things even better, my task was to organize the work of some guys who weren't under my responsibility, and I was pregnant.

So I got to experience a hostile work environment.

The pleasant daily interactions I had went something like this:

Or like this:

My point is this: in a situation like that, it would be legitimate to get angry and put the guy in his place.

Only when a woman gets angry, it causes this kind of reaction:

Insensitive comments

Here we go, she's off.

Exchanged glances

What do my clothes have to do with you?

Triumphant grin

This way of attacking a person, making them think that they're the ones reacting badly, it's a very practical technique for manipulating someone so that they don't rebel.

It's even got a name: "gaslighting."

Two things make it easier to gaslight a person or a group of people:

- solidarity among the dominant group (in my case, male solidarity)

- social conditioning that gives us a biased view of reality (in my case, the patriarchy incites us to view male aggressiveness as a legitimate way of asserting oneself, and female aggressiveness as hysteria).

The story of the suffragettes is a typical example of gaslighting. At the beginning of the 20th century, women didn't have the right to vote. So they weren't REALLY seen as autonomous human beings.

Autonomous

Nope.

All over Europe, women campaigned for this right without much success.

In 1903, the suffragette movement was created to move toward more violent forms of action, like, for example,

chaining themselves to public buildings,

burning down sites that represented male dominance,

or forcing their way into male assemblies.

These actions left many of them in jail.
  When they went on hunger strike, they were force-fed.

But we just want our rights!

They also organized demonstrations, during which they were harassed by the police.
  Groups of men pulled the protesters into alleyways and raped them. The police turned a blind eye.

And yet, what was criticized and talked about at the time wasn't the violence of depriving human beings of their rights. It wasn't the violence that was being used in an attempt to make them abandon their struggle either.

No, what was criticized was the violence of the suffragettes. In fact, I still hear these criticisms today.

In any case, we once again see the two features I mentioned: solidarity among the dominant group (men run the State, the police, and the justice system) and a context that creates a biased view. It seems normal that women can't vote: therefore, it's not a form of violence.

And the same thing is happening with uprisings today. Whether it's a worker who tears off the shirt of a manager who's ruining his life,

a protester who burns a luxury car,

or a neighborhood that goes up in flames the nth time that someone there dies from police shootings.

It's always the violence of the oppressed that fingers are pointed at.

So I'm wondering . . .
what level of humiliation,
what level of "legal"
violence do we have to
reach before it seems
legitimate for us to act
outside the boundaries
that our oppressors have
defined for us?

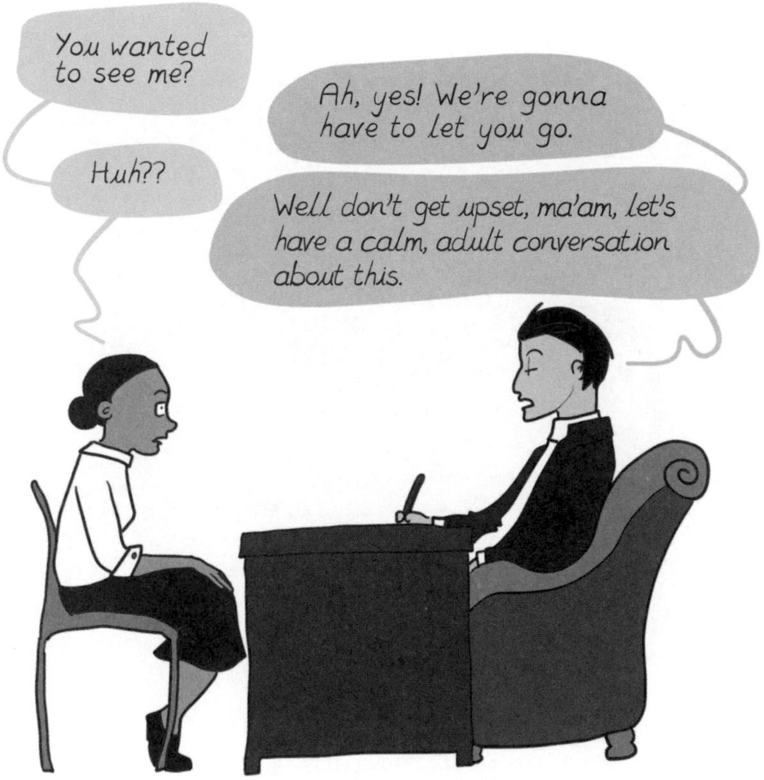
You wanted to see me?
Ah, yes! We're gonna have to let you go.
Huh??
Well don't get upset, ma'am, let's have a calm, adult conversation about this.

3
The Story of My Friend C.

I meet C. in a militant feminist group.
   We get along, we have a few drinks, and she tells me about her experience of childbirth.
   I'm flabbergasted, since I personally had a great experience.
   So I look into it, read reports, gather some figures.
   And I decide to talk about it.

My friend C. is funny and intelligent, she's got a strong character.

In 2007, C. has a baby in her belly.

C.'s baby.

She prepares diligently for the birth, it's a really important event for her. She picks a maternity ward that promotes natural childbirth, goes to all the classes, and reads about it extensively.

On September 11, her water breaks and she goes to the maternity ward. Her labor is drawn out, she spends many hours walking up and down the corridors with her partner. She asks to use the pool that was shown to her during the classes, but the staff doesn't take the time to bring her there.

After 20 hours, C. realizes that she's exhausting herself and that she needs an epidural to rest and to be able to push. There's one thing she dreads above all else: an episiotomy. She fears it so much that she made sure it was written in her file that she refused to have one.

The epidural works for a while, but then the pain returns. Despite everything, C. is ready to bring her baby into the world. She pushes for a long time. Both mother and baby are fine. And yet . . .

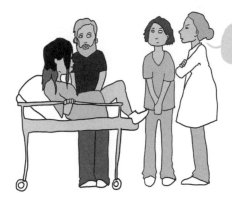

The baby is born, but C. is not happy. She feels mutilated. No one tells her, but at that moment, she hemorrhages. Her partner and baby are taken out, and she has stitches, and a manual examination of the uterus and rectum.

C. spends the weeks following the birth in tears. It took 13 stitches to sew up her episiotomy. The scar heals badly; her relationship and sex life are on the rocks.

It takes a long time and psychological help for her to come out of her depression.

Her well-prepared childbirth did not go down at all as she had hoped.

When I tell C.'s story to my friends, their reactions are unequivocal.

You're not a doctor.

She did what was best for the mother and baby.

They know better than we do! We have to leave it to them!

Only unlike my friends, C. knows that in reality an episiotomy is rarely necessary. Let's start by reminding ourselves of what it is:

Medio-lateral episiotomy

Midline episiotomy

It's an incision, a few centimeters long, along the lining of the vagina: the mucous membrane, the skin, and the perineum are cut.

Long considered a last resort, this practice became very popular in the 1920s.

Today, it's practiced on average in 30% of cases.

Different doctors give different reasons for doing them.

Only none of these explanations are grounded in scientific fact . . .

There's no link between the size of the baby's head and possible risk of injury.

And a narrow birth canal helps the baby clear out its respiratory tracts.

As for bad tearing . . . we've known for years that far from preventing it, episiotomies tend to make it worse. It's logical: it's always easier to tear something that's already been cut . . .

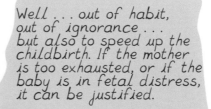

That's ridiculous, why would they keep doing it if it's not useful?

Well . . . out of habit, out of ignorance . . . but also to speed up the childbirth. If the mother is too exhausted, or if the baby is in fetal distress, it can be justified.

But sometimes they just need to free up the beds . . .

The truth is that we're not interested in the female genital organs beyond their reproductive role.

In 2005, the French National College of Gynecologists and Obstetricians had already concluded that there was no objective reason for such widespread episiotomies.

But we're reluctant to ask midwives and physicians to call their methods into question.

Citing the survival of the mother and baby is a good way to coerce us into accepting these practices . . . and we give over our bodies without discussion.

Yet all it takes is for people to be a bit more willing to improve the way things are done. For example, the maternity ward in the French town of Besançon practices episiotomies in less than 1% of cases.

The number of serious tears has been reduced.

And slight tears (which don't necessarily require stitches and heal much better) have increased: basically, they occur **instead** of episiotomies.

So, dear doctors, could you perhaps start considering that taking care of your patients is not JUST about keeping them alive?

It's also about doing all you can to avoid traumatizing their bodies . . .

. . . and minds.

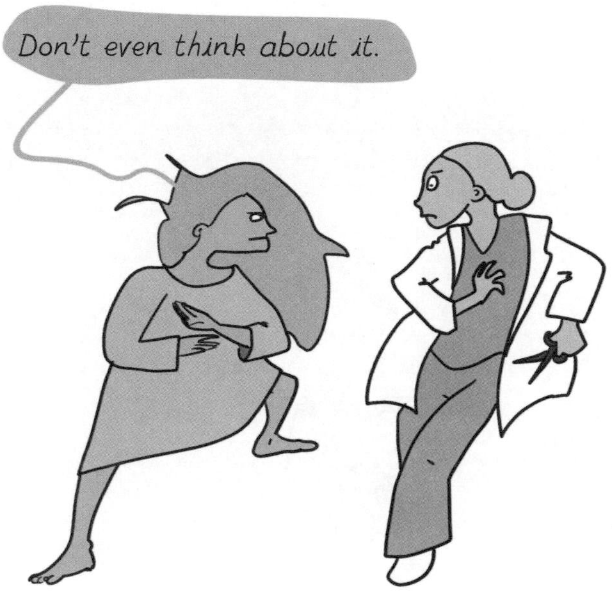
Don't even think about it.

4
The Male Gaze

The summer of 2016 is here and temperatures are rising.

It's time to get out some light clothes.

A colleague decides to tell me that he's happy with the display offered by our summer dresses.

I'm forced to explain that it's not especially meant for his pleasure.

In what kind of society do people feel entitled to think that women are there as eye candy for men?

A few years ago, I was chatting with a friend on the beach while a woman was bathing in front of us.

When she came out of the water, my friend looked repulsed.

Ew, cellulite!

That event really stands out in my mind because the girl overheard his remark, but it was neither the first nor the last time that I was witnessing this type of comment from a man.

They might have an opinion, fine, that's not really my problem.

But it becomes a problem when they feel that they're allowed to express their views publicly in every circumstance.

The thing is that all the media that we're engulfed by encourages us to observe and judge women's bodies. It's saturated with these images.

Whether in the movies,

in advertising,

in comics . . .

... or in video games.

In these universes, not only are women represented in a hyper-sexualized way . . .

. . . but often they don't have a real role, dialogue, or even a name. Basically, they're just there to provide the token tits.

So we often see them in completely improbable costumes and positions considering the context. Good luck fighting those zombies in your G-string.

And if you take a look at the previous images, you'll notice the frequent use of the "boobs-butt" position: completely unrealistic from an anatomical perspective, but allowing the viewer to ogle both at the same time!

And the worst part about all this is that since this universe is designed by and for a heterosexual male gaze . . .

. . . bit by bit, women themselves start to objectify each other. It's the attitude you're supposed to have to be "cool."

Personally, I've never seen the opposite scene play out. In fact, when I point out a good-looking guy to a male friend, his reaction is always "I wouldn't know, I'm straight."

Hey, take a look at that chick over there!

Hey, check out that dude!

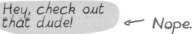
← Nope.

So we've seen how women's bodies are often depicted in a depersonalized way, for the pleasure of a viewer presumed to be male and straight. Now we get to the phase:

Okay, let's admit that. So what's the problem with looking at women?

Well, in fact, it's really annoying.

The fact that leering at women has been institutionalized to such a degree poses lots of problems.

First of all, viewers with an overlooked gender or sexual orientation have to adapt, either by imagining themselves in undervalued roles, or by giving up their own identity to project themselves onto male, heterosexual characters. Yet from a very young age, we construct the characters with whom we identify. So it's a problem to have to choose between being the eye candy or the standard straight male, if that's not our identity.

And then, like my friend on the beach, men are used to scrutinizing and commenting on women's bodies. They have a hard time seeing us from another angle.

It's evident at work: when female candidates come in for interviews, the first comments are always about whether or not they're nice to look at.

And as we well know from experience, we can never catch a break. Whether it's out on the street, on the subway or bus, at work, or when we're out for the evening, we know we're being looked at, and that means we can't loosen up and focus on what we've got to do.

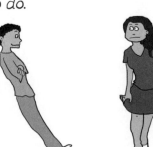

In fact, many studies have shown that the feeling of being observed had a negative impact on women, on their self-confidence and their intellectual capacities.

It's even been shown that we've integrated the male gaze to such an extent that we feel like we're being watched even when we're alone . . .

A number of studies, including one done in 2012 at the Free University of Brussels, have attempted to analyze how our brain functions when we recognize something.

In fact, we don't identify objects and people in the same way. We recognize an object through the details that make it up, but when it comes to a person, we'll look at how these details come together to form a whole.

And, well, the researchers showed that while we did indeed look at men as human beings, women were analyzed in the same way as objects, regardless of the observer's gender.

But while we **interact** with a person, we **use** an object.

And seeing women as objects poses obvious problems in terms of respect and consent.

Okay, the good news is that the researchers also showed that the way we look at women changes when they are placed in a context where it's easier to recognize them as a whole person.

So it's far from being a foregone conclusion, it's totally possible to move beyond it.

I therefore suggest doing all we can to stop visually dismembering women. It would allow everyone to think about far more interesting things!

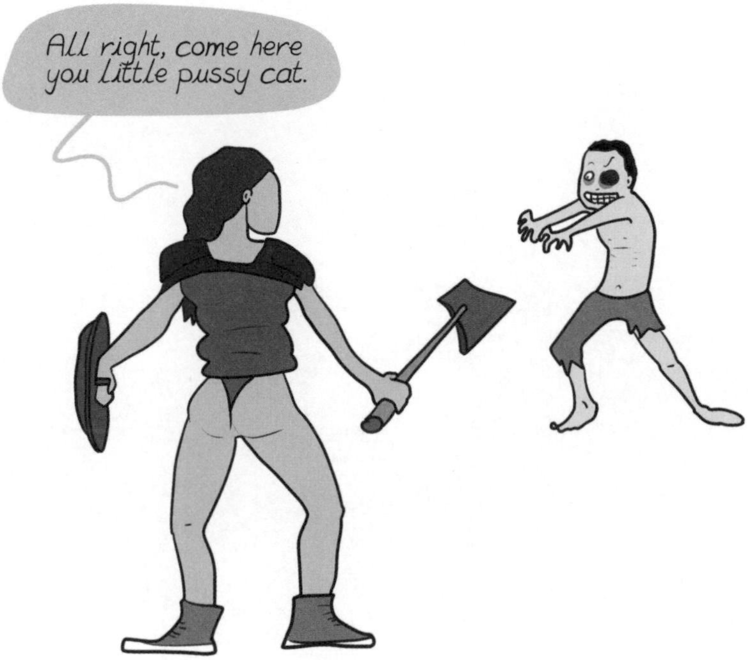
All right, come here you little pussy cat.

5
Show Me That Bosom

I grew up in France. In my family and in those of my friends, we had certain customs that I never questioned until I came here. In summer, the men of the family would go around bare-chested. Little girls were (tacitly) allowed to do it too until their breasts grew out. As women, we would systematically wear T-shirts to cover our chest.

* Translator's note: A made-up country.

To go bathing, we didn't wear swimming trunks like our male friends. We used this practical piece of clothing called a "swimsuit," which could be made up of one or two pieces and came in many colors. This allowed us to go swimming and to play in the water, without worrying about revealing our mysterious nipples.

I never saw this custom as a form of oppression.
   Even if it may seem crazy in the eyes of my new compatriots, my mother and father got along very well, I had a happy childhood, and I was never told that my body was dirty or that the only future I could hope for was to raise a family and stay in the kitchen.

When I arrived in Maristan, I was delighted to discover a country that held women's rights in such high regard. It was explained to me that women's nipples were not any more shameful than those of men, and that what was shameful was forcing us to hide them. I rather agreed.

Only it was difficult for me to all of a sudden uncover my breasts, which I had always kept hidden. So I continued to wear bras and T-shirts, even though Maristan was a very hot country.

I wasn't really the only one, since in my neighborhood, many French and European immigrants continued to do so.

Sometimes, out of nostalgia, we got together to sew "breast covers" as they call them here, since the only shop selling bras that a friend had set up was closed by the authorities.

I never told my daughter that a woman's breasts were a temptation for men.

I let her learn at school that all human beings were equal, despite their physiological differences.

When she asked me why I didn't show my chest, I simply replied: "a question of habit."

One day, my daughter reached the age when your body changes, your hips widen, and the first curves appear.

She started her period and it was me, not her father, who helped her navigate this phase.

Her breasts appeared and she constantly looked at them, touching them, both proud and panicked. When she ran, they bounced, and it wasn't very practical when she played basketball, even though it gave her a strange feeling of lightness.

One day, she came to see me with a serious expression, and she asked me for a bra.

I was stunned.

I remembered the day I had asked my own mother the same thing.

Well, in my case it was for a different reason.

I was still flat-chested but I wanted to act all grown up, to make the boys like me, because it's true that in my country, young girls were quickly encouraged to make their body attractive, we called it "being sexy."

When Lola asked me this, I didn't know how to react.

I didn't want her friends to make fun of her or reject her, but she insisted, assuring me that she would feel more comfortable and that her friends would accept her as she was.

I sewed her a bra and told her, laughing, that among women we called it a "boulder holder."

She felt both disconcerted and proud when she tried it on.
I think that she thought back to the photos of her ancestors, and that seeing herself with this piece of clothing brought her closer to her roots.

She asked me for a T-shirt to wear over it, and to cover her rounded belly and her underarm hair.

I told her that it was too much, that she would be seen as advocating nationalist terrorism, and that she needed to learn to be comfortable with her body.

She went off to school with her new bra. I let her go with a lump in my throat, praying that this country would keep its promise of tolerance and let her study in peace.

I made her memorize a good comeback if anyone bothered her:
"I don't need my nipples to learn."

I worried all day and restlessly awaited her return.
  She came back dejected, her head hung low.

Mom, it was a nightmare. It's not my friends who bothered me, it was the teachers!

I swear, Mom, they ruined my day. They told me I was perpetuating a practice that was archaic and incompatible with the values of Maristan.

That I could feel proud of my family's origins and traditions, but that I had to observe them at home.

That I was an intelligent girl and that they were disappointed by my choice. That I could have "made something of myself" but that I had decided to "go down the wrong path."

I felt terrible and held her in my arms. I didn't know whether I should tell her to stay strong and ignore their bullshit, or whether I was better off telling her to forget about the bra and that everything would be fine.

She made the decision for herself.
She chose to turn this piece of
fabric into a fight.

The problem is that the past few years have left a dark stain on the history of Maristan. People feel exasperated by the French.
    They insist that they can't stand the smell of cheese seeping out of their apartments. They keep complaining that we speak too loud. We're being urged to spend Christmas in silence after several complaints about excessive noise in the evening of December 24, 2039.*

NOTICE: NO NOISE AT CHRISTMAS

*Translator's note: This narrative takes place in an imagined future where the situation in France has gotten so bad that the stream of immigration has reversed and Europeans are emigrating South.

So Lola had picked a bad time to start wearing her bra. What's more, other girls her age started to do the same in schools across the country.

She fought several times with teachers who wanted to dissuade her, "for her own good," as they said.

The worst were the women, so proud to show off their beautiful breasts that they spent hours dolling up in the morning and tanning in the evening after work.

One day, Lola answered back, saying that if they were really so free and equal, they wouldn't be spending so much time trying to appeal to men, and that above all, there would be more women in parliament.

She was given an hour of detention.

When she gave me the report card to sign, I couldn't help but smile with pride.

What a courageous young woman she was!

After months of problems and arguments with the teaching staff, during which I was called in numerous times to remind them that this was her choice and that she felt better this way . . .

. . . during which my husband was investigated to check whether he was being influenced by European extremist networks . . .

. . . I believed that it would just be a matter of weeks before this whole thing blew over. But the state of Maristan decided to forbid bras in schools. Any girl who refused to abide by the law would be expelled.

I asked Lola to take it off.

She didn't want to hear it and was utterly miserable. She thought she could win her case and that her victory would make her a heroine.

She continued to go to school in a bra, thinking that they would never expel a top student whose work was constantly lauded.

And it was true, they didn't want to expel her. They said that it would be a loss "for you and for us."

They wanted to force her to remove it.

So one day, in history class, the teacher made her come up to the front and took off her bra. In front of everyone. Of course, the students weren't shocked to see breasts since they saw them all day long. But Lola felt naked, humiliated, and insulted.

These emotions made her nipples harden spontaneously, which made her even more uncomfortable. A classmate even thought it appropriate to stretch out his hand to touch her.

They've sure grown since 6th grade!

Today, my daughter's no longer going to school. We don't go to the beach anymore, despite the heat waves, because they're forbidden to women who cover their bosoms. We get together with the local women, cook quiches, and drink liters of red wine.

When we go to the store, people scowl at us with our shopping carts full of cheese.
    Once, a policeman threw an insult at me while I was crossing the street.

I think back to those Sunday barbecues when my father, bare-chested, kindled the flames, and my mother carefully set out the vegetables on a plate.

Sure, it was all very gender-conforming behavior, as we now say. I'm glad that my daughter knows how to light a fire and that my son likes to garnish the serving plates.

But shit, at least we could all go to the beach.

6
The Wonderful Tale of Mohamed

Following the terrorist attacks in Paris, at the end of 2015 police raids were rife. The state of emergency meant that around 3,000 homes were raided, their doors broken down in the middle of the night. Whole families were held at gunpoint and searched, often for reasons that had nothing to do with terrorism.

I'm in the metro, listening to a French cultural radio show, and I hear Mohamed talk about how the police destroyed his building in the middle of the night.

Mohamed is 27 years old. He's Egyptian.

He paints houses for a living.

He shares a studio apartment with his friend, on rue Corbillon, in the Paris suburb of Saint-Denis.

On November 18, 2015, Mohamed and his friend are asleep in their studio apartment.

At 4 a.m., they're startled awake by the sound of explosions.

Mohamed goes to open the window and sees lots of police officers in the building opposite his.

The officers shout to him to open the other shutter, which he quickly does.

Then he places his hands on his head.

And he's shot at and wounded.

He and his friend get very scared and run away.

They hide in the bathroom.

Until 10 a.m., so for 6 whole hours.

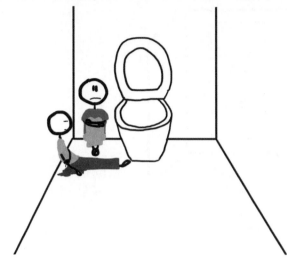

At 10 a.m., the police break down the door of their studio apartment.

They point their weapons at Mohamed and his friend, pull down their pants and underwear with their feet, make them get out onto the street, and push them up against a wall to be searched.

Once he's been searched, an ambulance picks up Mohamed to stop the bleeding and take him to a hospital.

At the hospital, police officers cuff Mohamed's arm and leg to the bed and question him . . .

... for four days, without telling him why he's being held there.

On Saturday, they tell Mohamed that he's free to go and send him back "home."

Since then, Mohamed and his friend have been staying in a 100-square-foot hotel room. Mohamed can no longer work since he can't use his arm.

And they risk being deported since a number of victims of the Saint-Denis raid were issued an official order to leave French territory.

Following the raid, their building is un-
inhabitable.

Only 6 families out of 50 were found
new places to live.

The residents are traumatized; children
sleep in their clothes since they're scared
they might have to get out of their house
in the middle of the night.

A few people who owned their apart-
ments continue to pay the bills for a
building that was destroyed, and they
don't have the means to find somewhere
else to stay.

Isn't it wonderful, this land of freedom?

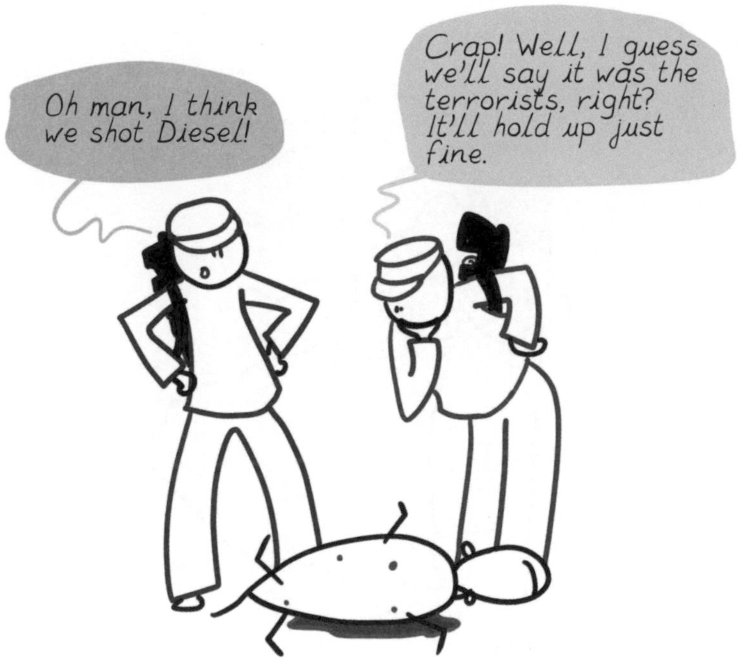
Oh man, I think we shot Diesel!
Crap! Well, I guess we'll say it was the terrorists, right? It'll hold up just fine.

7
The Wait

My boyfriend and I were always careful not to encroach upon each other's freedoms.

Both of us were able to go out as we pleased.

We never complained.

Well . . .

. . . almost never.

When we had our child and I started working again, we organized things like most couples:

My boyfriend dropped the baby off at childcare in the morning,

and I picked him up in the evening.

For me, like for many other women, that meant leaving work a lot earlier than before...

Aaaargh... okay, never mind, I'm off.

CLAP

...which often meant leaving a task unfinished...

. . . and giving up on after-work drinks with colleagues.

Leaving earlier did not mean working less.

It just meant carefully organizing my day to get as many things done in as short a time as possible.

All the while **still** being considered a slacker.

Yet when I got home, it's not as if I could relax.

Every evening was just about making it through with the last grain of available energy,

to survive until the life-saving return of my boyfriend.

Which sometimes involved a painful wait.

When they become mothers, most women give up their free evenings . . .

but for fathers, this is less often the case.

My friend M. told me about reaching the edge of despair

when one day she heard the sound of keys in the door and thought her shift was over . . .

only to have her partner, upon walking in an hour late, proudly announce as he kicked off his shoes:

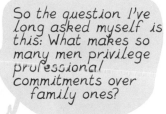

Of course, this impression of "not having time" is very subjective . . .

. . . since we manage to find that time to go pick up our children.

So the question I've long asked myself is this: What makes so many men privilege professional commitments over family ones?

Obviously, if lives are at stake, it's not the same issue.

Okay, well I'm done here.

Aaaaaaaaaargh

The same goes when someone is barely earning a living

and needs to work late just to get by.

And yet, in every job I've had, I've seen many fathers grant them-selves flexible schedules,

with decent lunch breaks,

heated hallway discussions,

and not always focusing on work . . .

. . . and leaving the office at 8 p.m. to "get the job finished."

What we quickly realize with regards to this after-school period, and what most fathers don't get, is that once you're a parent, staying on to finish your work is a form of **comfort**: not a **duty** or a **gallant feat**.

Pleasant feeling of accomplishment = personal comfort!

In fact, our society still applies two different value scales to men and women.

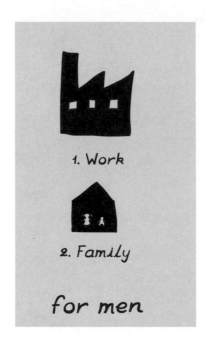

1. Work

2. Family

for men

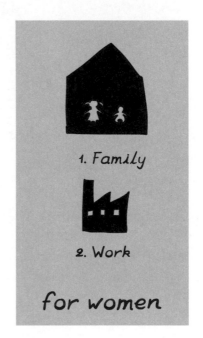

1. Family

2. Work

for women

So by giving up their time for their company, men have a greater sense of *accomplishing their duty* . . .

. . . than by *leaving early* to be with their family.

And what's more, in France, the **time spent at work** is seen as more important than the **work effectively accomplished.**

Joseph sent me an e-mail at midnight last night!

Whoooa . . .

So yesterday, as I was leaving work at 10 p.m., I thought to myself . . .

That means that to get noticed, promoted, and rewarded, employees have to display, not their ability to **work efficiently,**

Goodnight, boss!

but their willingness to **sacrifice personal time** (and therefore family time) for the benefit of their employer.

We more or less accept that women, once they become mothers, give up this behavior.

Even if the result is that we give up all hope of seeing our careers and our salaries progress.

For men, this is still looked down upon.

We find ourselves forced into positions . . .

. . . where on the one hand,
women fulfill a role
that is meaningful
but exhausting, undervalued,
and costly in terms of
career and salary . . .

. . . while on the other hand,
men tend to remain stuck
in an attitude of presenteeism,
which is senseless,
but which provides them
with financial and
professional opportunities.

To get out of this position, we have to find
a way to break down these barriers.

And for that, we need to call into question how we order our respective values.

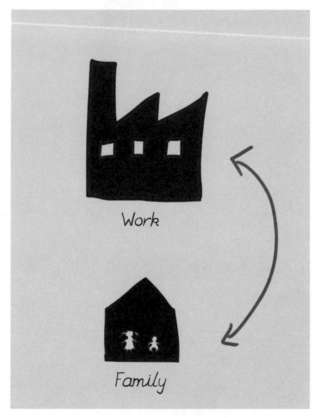

Work

Family

For me, these are the ones that need to be reversed.

Since for all of us, our **personal and family time** should be at the top of our list of what we value, and our time at work **merely a means by which to achieve this**.

Let's combat presenteeism!

Let's stop encouraging the idea of sacrificing our free time for the companies we work for.

And *Let's work less!*

You'll be asking: But how can I work less when I need the money to feed my family?

And that's something I've pondered for a long time.

So in the next chapter, I'll tell you about how I came to realize that we could live better by working less.

Lots of hugs and kisses, and now go spend some time with your little ones!

8
Work!

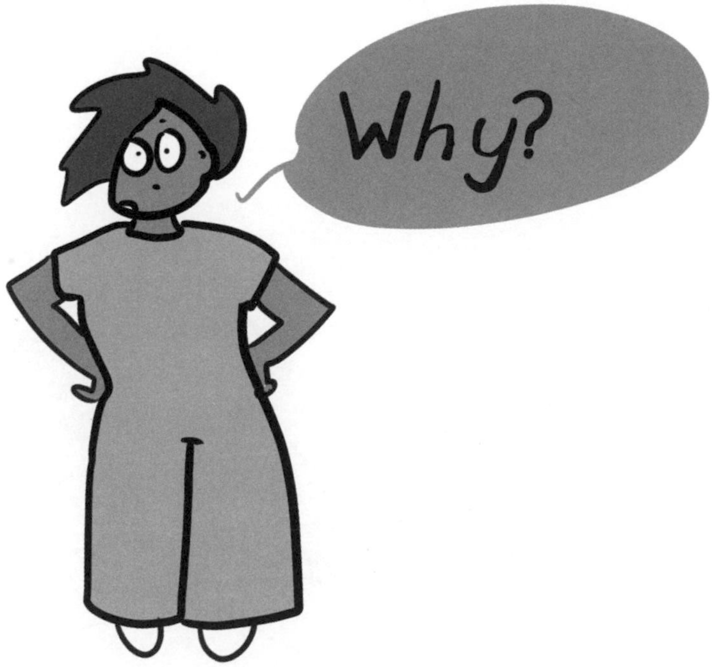
Why?

In the last chapter, I talked about how all the time we spend at work doesn't allow us to lead a serene life at home.

In this one, I want to tell you about how I realized that we could all live differently.

And to do this, I'll start by describing my typical day at work.

On workdays, I wake up at 7 a.m.

Huh, already?

RING RING RING . . .
RING RING RING . . .

I don't have time to eat before leaving the house,
or to see my son, who's still asleep.

To get to work, I take three modes of transportation:
the metro, then the tram, then another metro.

Since there's many of us, I stay standing.

Once I get to the office, I take my place so that everyone can clearly see what time I've arrived.

Then I go get a coffee and come back to start working on my tasks.

My tasks aren't uninteresting, but they haven't changed in ten years,

so most of the time, I'm a bit bored.

At noon, we've got one hour for lunch, so we have to eat quickly.

Some of us bring sandwiches and others don't even eat.
We're told off if we take longer than we should.

Once we've gulped down our lunch, we go back to the office and I go back to my tasks,

waiting to be able to leave to pick up my son.

I go through this routine every day,

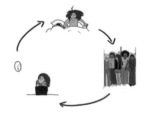 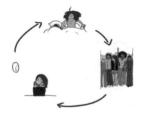

5 days a week.

For the past 10 years.

And while I'm well aware that I'm lucky to have a job in which I'm not being

paid minimum wage,

doing dangerous tasks,

or being overworked,

the idea of keeping going like this until I'm 65

tends to depress me a bit. I don't know if you feel the same.

I was resigned to it: I was always told that the only society we could live in was one in which we had the choice

between working our butts off every day for years . . .

. . . or being out of work, facing financial difficulties, and spending our time between the unemployment and welfare offices.

Please could you show up at the unemployment office before last week, we have a position to offer you 200 miles from where you live. Otherwise you're out. Kisses.

I realized that we were being taken for a ride while watching a program about universal income.

No waaaaaay . . .

I found out about the concept of **bullshit jobs.**

Bullshit jobs are those that serve no real purpose, that contribute nothing to humanity, nor to the planet.

But despite this, they continue to exist and to take up entire days in people's lives for years on end.

To find out whether you're doing a bullshit job, it's simple: imagine it disappearing

and ask yourself what impact that would have on society.

I asked myself this very question: I spent 12 years of my career developing software that allows companies to be more competitive than the next.

And then later, since I worked as a contractor, I went on to develop the same thing for another company.

I could have spent these 12 years at work playing checkers

without it making a darn bit of difference to humanity.

Take away the work done by nurses, bus drivers, or artists, and the impact on humanity will be evident.

But take away the work of a trader, a tax adviser, an advertising executive, or a financial journalist ... and what will happen?

Nothing.

The sun will still rise, we'll still be able to eat and sleep, and the hospitals will keep running

just like before.

In the program I watched, sociologist and economist Bernard Friot estimated that 30% of all jobs are bullshit jobs. That's when I realized:

Hm . . . in fact . . .

We don't need to work more! It's the opposite . . .

Task automation allowed us to get rid of lots of painful jobs, while producing more.

We already produce so much food that half gets thrown away,

and there is more empty housing than there are homeless people.

If people starve and sleep on the street, it's not because there's not enough food or lodging, it's because it's not **evenly distributed**.

And in reality, even during the postwar boom when everything had to be rebuilt, not everybody had a job!

Um, yes. Who do you think appeared on the job market in the last 50 years?

Job market

Hmm?
Job market

WE did!
Women!
Job market

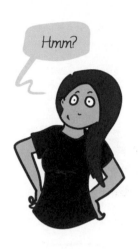

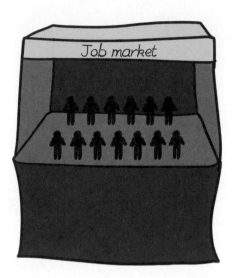

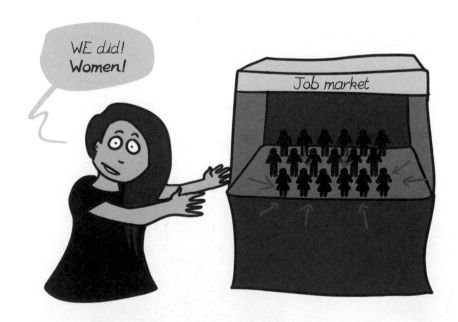

Since 1960, the number of "active"* women went up from 40% to 80%....

So ... since we automated many tasks, and since so many more of us have a job ...well, we should all be working **a lot less**.

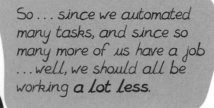

We should have reduced the number of working hours and brought down the retirement age ...

*That's not to say that we weren't working. But we were only working at home, and for free.

Instead of that, we keep slaving away, while others are unemployed, or doing bullshit jobs.

So why do we force people to work so much if it's useless?

We might say that it's to "make our economy work" . . .

But what's the point of "making our economy work," if it's not working for us?

A war,

or a car accident,

those are really great for the economy.

Yum!

On the other hand,

caring for the sick,

looking after children . . .

. . . the economy doesn't like that much.
It thinks of these as "loads" or "expenses."

Do we really
need books?

In fact, we continue to work our butts off for only one reason:
because it increases the wealth of those for whom we're working.

To put things simply, let's take the example of George, a factory owner, who
would like to manufacture something.

Maybe I could manufacture
something . . .

George talks to his shareholders.

And there you have it. It's more lucrative for George to make a bullshit product than something useful.

Profit and humanity don't go hand in hand.

To manufacture his bullshit product, George will hire employees.

And he'll sell it for a lot more than what it cost to make.

> But . . . I made it for one dollar!

> Yes, sure! But it's MY factory.

Just because he owns the factory.

This is called **Lucrative** property: i.e., when we possess things not because we need them to live, but because we want to use them to get rich.

Of course, it's more complicated for small business owners, small farmers, or small shopkeepers who can barely keep their business afloat, but the same principle applies.

George will have become rich without creating anything useful, and without working. He's just taken the money generated by his employees.

In 1990, 30% of the value created by our work was already taken by owners.

30%

70%

30% for the owners
70% for the workers

And today, that's actually gone up to 40%.

For them, it will never be enough, and we're still just as poor!

Since, even though we produce more thanks to automation,

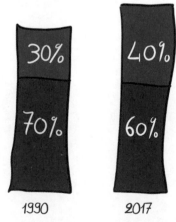

30%

70%

1990

40%

60%

2017

it's the owners who benefit, we don't.

But *I* took the **risks**! I put my big balls on the line by opening this factory!

Insolent little woman.

George, you **inherited** your factory. And in any case, when big companies are in trouble, the government helps them out. And with **our taxes!** **We're** the ones who take on that risk, not you.

Since I understood this, what I believe is that this system will never generate anything positive for us.

Factories should not be there to make their owners rich, but simply to respond to our needs.

So I don't think that they should belong to one person, but to a community. A bit like a co-op.

That way, we could decide together what bullshit jobs we could get rid of.

(Personally, I would vote against, but hey, being part of a community means that everyone has a say!)

Once all the bullshit jobs have been identified and removed,

we can spend more time on tasks that are useful to people, like caregiving and education.

And above all, we could **work a lot less.**

And of course, working less would not mean living less well.

Once we're rid of all the bullshit jobs, everything useful would still be produced,

housing,

food,

entertainment,

and there would be enough of it for everyone.

Only there would no longer be any owners who get rich on the sidelines.

Pfff...

Sorry, George.

So of course, the owners themselves don't see it that way.

They do everything they can to make you believe that society cannot exist without them

and that, for us, the only possible way of life is to slave away until death (or just about).

More and more of us are thinking along these lines, and it should be encouraged.

It's a huge topic, there's a lot more to say. But at least it's a start!

Of course, we're stirring up trouble, so our voices aren't very present in the media. But we're there.

To learn more, you can start by searching online for information about universal income. I hope you'll find it all as fascinating as I do.

The more of us there are out there, the faster things will change!

It's still summer and activism has dwindled.

The demonstrations and "Nuit Debout" social movement* were obliterated by the violence of state and police repression.

My mind is somewhere else, and I decide to talk about one of my top anatomical discoveries: the clitoris!

*Translator's note: roughly translated as "Up All Night," this social movement took place in France in 2016 as a reaction against new labor laws.

9
Check Your Pussy

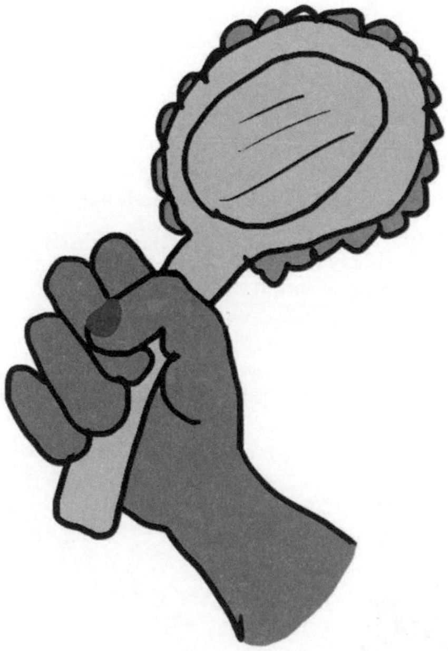

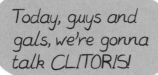 Today, guys and gals, we're gonna talk CLITORIS!

 That thing we discover more or less late, since no one tells us about it in school.

I don't know if you've already taken a mirror to have a look at all that's going on down there, but until recently, I actually thought that the clitoris was also used to pee.

 A bit like a cock!

I'll skip the details, but a few
clues along those lines made
me wonder, and I went to check.

So for those who are a bit oblivious like me,
this is what a pussy looks like:

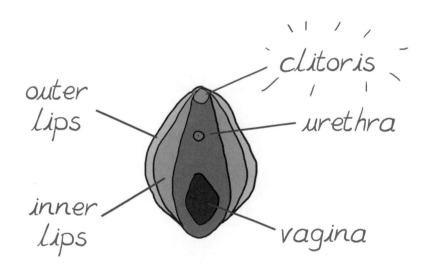

So how can something so small create an
intergalactic tsunami in your whole body?

Well, because this little thing is just
the ROOT of something much bigger.
Something almost tentacular.

If you're
scared of
spiders, hang
in there, I've
drawn you a
clitoris.

TADAAAAAA

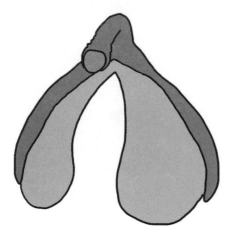

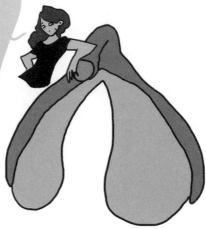

That's the glans right there (the part that sticks out).

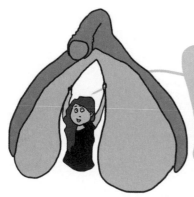

Here I am between the bulbs of the vestibule where we usually find the vaginal opening.

HiPS.

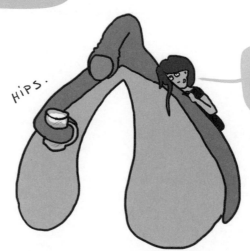

And here are the crura.

135

And that's how such a small-but-in-fact-very-big thing can bring you so much pleasure, without the need to always caress the visible part.

Once the glans is stimulated, the bulbs become engorged and can provoke sensations during vaginal and anal penetration.

The so-called vaginal orgasm therefore doesn't come from the vagina, but from the internal part of the clitoris.

And many people don't experience it, because our sensitivity depends on many factors . . .

It's believed that the sensations we feel could be linked to Skene's glands. They can be found in variable numbers all along the urethra,

Urethra

Skene's glands

birth canal

clitoris root

and they are thought to be the source of female ejaculation.

Not to be confused with vaginal lubrication, secreted by cells in the vaginal walls during sexual arousal.

It could also depend on the complexity of the network of nerves, blood vessels, and muscles in and around the clitoris.

In short, the truth is that we really don't know much about it.

And we don't know much for a very good reason: nobody cares!

Sniff. After everything I do for you.

And yet we've known about the clitoris since the 16th century. At that time, people thought that women had to orgasm to get pregnant. Suffice to say that these gentlemen had to make a bit of effort.

Only, bit by bit, people began to worry that these ladies were a bit too happy to forego the penis altogether.

So masturbation was prohibited, and female circumcision appeared.

In 19th-century Germany, they would completely remove the clitoris of little girls who were tempted to caress themselves.

Then, in the 20th century, people realized that orgasms had nothing to do with fertility.

So the word "clitoris" completely disappeared from the dictionary.

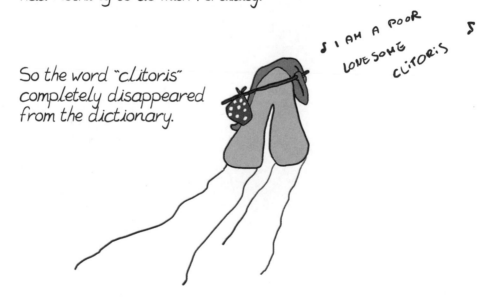

Freud decreed that the clitoral orgasm was that of little girls, and that real women only came through penetration.

So where do we stand today?

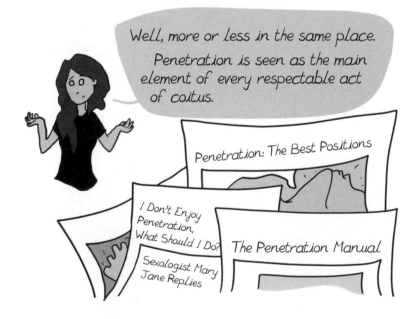

The clitoris finds itself in the blind spot of all scientific literature and is completely absent from school texts.

Why be interested in an organ that's "not useful"?

That's what's going on with the scientists. And with the rest of humanity?

Well, it's no different. In 2002, Shere Hite updated the report on sexuality that she had published in 1976: nothing has changed.

Among other things, she notes that:
- 95% of women reach orgasm through masturbation, but only 44% with their partner.
- 64% of women consider that their partner is indifferent to their pleasure.
- And over 70% of women do not reach orgasm through penetration.

In 2009, Annie Sautivet, an art teacher, asked 300 of her 13- and 14-year-old students to draw the female genital organs. Most were not able to place the clitoris correctly.

Half of all girls in 8th grade and 25% of those in 9th grade didn't know they had one.

It's not very surprising, seeing as nothing is done to help us learn more.

We possess the only organ fully devoted to sexual pleasure, and nobody cares!

So maybe it's time to go get a mirror and explore all of this with (or without!) our partners . . .

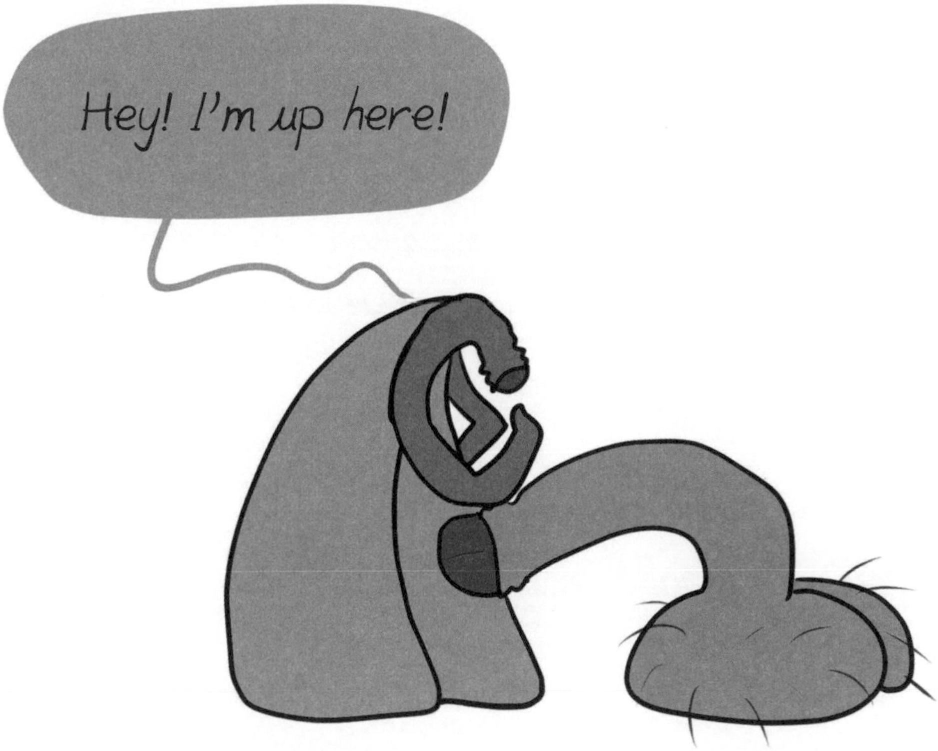
Hey! I'm up here!

In July, 24-year-old Adama Traore becomes yet another victim of police violence.

My mind is back, and I decide to talk about the dozens of people who perish at the hands of the police each year.

10
Just Another Guy
from the Hood

Adama is 24. He lives in
Beaumont-sur-Oise, a
small town north of Paris.

On July 19, his birthday, he's going for a walk
in town when policemen appear to pick up his
brother, Bagui.

Adama doesn't have his ID on him.
He tries to run away.

The police catch him. He cries out and
surrenders to them, but they still hit him
over the head, cuff him, and throw him
into the back of the police van.

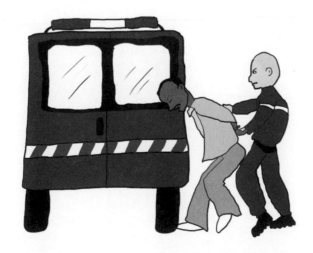

Bagui is taken to the police station separately. When he arrives, he sees Adama handcuffed, lying motionless on the ground. He tries to intervene, so he's taken to another police station.

At 9 p.m., Adama's family are told that he lost consciousness. They go to the hospital.

So they go to the police station.

At 11 p.m., they're finally told that Adama died while being transported to the station.

According to the prosecutor, Adama lost consciousness in the police van, first aid was called in, but they could do nothing.

Yet a number of witnesses affirm that they never saw first aid arrive, and that they saw Adama being hit on the head while he was handcuffed and lying on the floor of the police station.

The next day, his family shows up at the police station to see the body, but they're driven away with tear gas.

The autopsy reveals "no significant signs of violence" and "a serious infection," yet Adama seemed in perfect health according to many witnesses.

So?

Well, he's got a cold and signs of blows to the head.

Perfect, we'll go with "no significant signs" and "a serious infection."

Scene from my overblown imagination

If we take this story on its own, the difference between the police version and the witnesses' version could just leave us perplexed.

My wife always said, when it seems suspicious, it probably is.

Only Adama is far from being the only person to die while being transported by the police.

In 2014, Hocine Bouras died from a gunshot wound to the head while being taken to court. He had allegedly tried to take an officer's weapon. Hocine was handcuffed at the time.

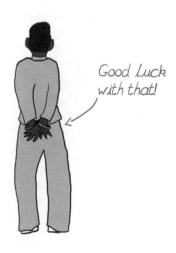

Good Luck with that!

In another case in 2014, Abdelhak Goradia died from a "heart attack" while being driven to the airport to be deported to Algeria.

Oops.

Unlike the US, France provides no statistics on the number of people killed by the police.

But many associations try to do this, and they estimate the number to be between 10 and 15 dead per year.

They're mainly young men from disadvantaged areas, with North African or sub-Saharan origins.

Each case follows a similar scenario.

A young man dies during an arrest.

If it's by bullet wounds, the police officer pleads legitimate defense.

Otherwise they report a loss of consciousness or heart attack.

It's radio silence on the part of the media, unless the case blows up, for example if riots break out.

In that case, they focus on the deceased man's past run-ins with the law.

The police version of the story will be relayed, and doubts cast on that of witnesses.

Like the media, the government will mince words to avoid talking about a police blunder.

It's a far cry from their firm condemnation of the act of ripping off someone's shirt.*

Prime Minister Shocked by Unjustifiable Acts of Physical Violence

The Republicans Demand HARSH Sanctions

*Translator's note: This refers to an event in 2015 when two Air France HR directors had their shirts torn off by employees angry at the prospect of losing their jobs.

In terms of judicial follow-up,

it's estimated that no further action is taken in 40% of cases.

Suspended prison sentences are often given out.

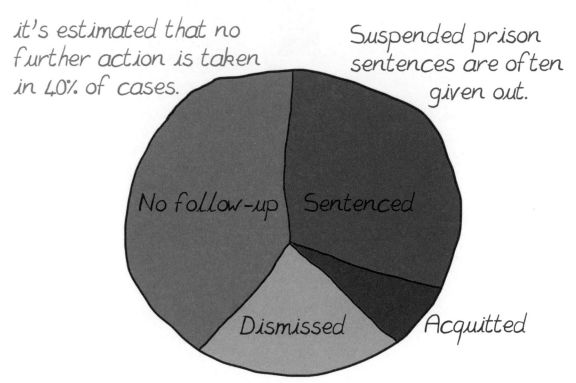

No follow-up   Sentenced

Dismissed   Acquitted

If there is a follow-up, the legal process takes many years, draining the families both financially and emotionally.

What I'm puzzled by is that many of these deaths occur during accidents as someone attempts to flee a police check.

For a long time, my reaction was the same as that of everyone who doesn't live in a disadvantaged area.

If he's running away, it must be for a reason.

But a person who is running away doesn't deserve to die any more than anyone else.

We have a legal system that's supposed to take care of that.

And what's more, the young men who run away often have nothing to feel guilty about.

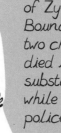

In the case of Zyed and Bouna, these two children died in a power substation while fleeing a police check.

One of their friends made a comment to a French journalist that really stuck with me.

"Today, if an officer approaches you for a police check, what do you do?"

"I run. When a policeman comes, you don't think about it, you run."

So when children are less scared of running into a power substation than of the police chasing after them, we might start wondering who the police are protecting . . .

Tired of being stopped by the police 5 times a day?
Sick of being held in custody?

A gift that's
just for you:
a cut-out white
man costume!

11
Chill Out

Hey, chill out a little!
Calm down, we're just kidding!
Have you already heard something like this after getting annoyed about some inappropriate comment or behavior?
I have, often.

For example, there was that time in school when I was finishing a team project.

It was a reflex answer, I didn't think about it.

Well, in the end, I was the one who had to apologize.

It happened a bunch of times during my teenage years.

Each time, it was my defensive reaction, rather than the attack, that seemed misplaced.

And in the end, I was in the wrong.

Was I just too sensitive to accept such jokes and "advice"?

Let's call a spade a spade: making an offended person believe that they're the ones at fault, that's **emotional manipulation**.

And we tend to lose our bearings if we're regularly subjected to it.

It's so humiliating to have to apologize for being hurt, that over time . . .

We stop reacting to these provocations altogether.

Today, like many women, I've become incapable of identifying the situations in which I have a right to be angry.

This social control of our emotions begins in childhood.

For boys, aggressiveness is considered normal very early on. It's one of the personality traits seen as necessary to "become a man."

Later on, they'll pay dearly for this stereotype.

First of all, because those that don't fit the mold, considered "not real men," will undergo many humiliations . . .

In fourth grade, my friend J. had a whole urine-filled bottle thrown at him because he was "playing girly games."

. . . and also because the others, to avoid meeting the same fate, try to display their virility through violent and risk-prone behavior.

That same year, my classmate S. lost a testicle while "play-fighting."

Little girls don't have these problems because any display of aggression is quickly checked.

What on earth are you doing to that poor dolly?

Throughout their lives, they'll be encouraged to remain gentle, and any aggressiveness will be portrayed as unseemly.

Once they're grown up, we'll refer to a woman who gets angry as **emotional** and **irrational**, since her reaction is not perceived as normal.

It's always going to be because we're on our period . . .

. . . or because we've got "a problem."

But the problem will always be in our head or in our body, never coming from the outside.

We've even come up with specific vocabulary for women who get angry. Like, for example, "hysterical," which comes from the word "uterus," created just for us!

So when you get angry, what's that called?

I'm "affirming my charisma"!

Or the famous "shrew," a term once used for women who had the nerve to refuse to do all the work around the house.

Well you look super angry!

Woah! Here it comes! . . .

We don't really want to be seen as hysterical or as pains in the ass. So in the end we bite our tongue . . .

...or express our emotions in a convoluted, restrained way, so that we don't come across as aggressive.

Sometimes we even say the exact opposite of what we're feeling.

Now, I'm not saying that the aim should be to start screaming at each other . . .

But channeling anger doesn't mean stifling it.

For a start, because it always ends up boomeranging back on us . . .

The body will physically manifest suppressed emotions: stress, depression, anxiety, and eating disorders are common among teenagers.

... and above all, because it's a **healthy** emotion to have in reaction to all sorts of things that we endure: lack of respect, provocations, or physical and verbal aggression.

And being used to stifling this signal leaves us paralyzed in situations when we're being attacked,

since we no longer trust our defensive instincts.

We perform a complex balancing act every day, stuck between commands to stand up for ourselves and accusations of hysteria when we do.

We walk this tightrope in all aspects of our lives: at home, out in society, and of course in the workplace.

It's evident in the political arena: men can shout, swear, and gesticulate

without the risk of being called hysterical or criticized for their ugly expressions.

It even helps them to be convincing and to get elected.

For women, these options just aren't on the table.

Did you see that amusing interview with a Trump supporter?

Female politicians are aware of these stereotypes, and they adapt.
No female candidate would risk yelling . . .

Because while anger affirms male charisma, it makes women seem less credible. And men are very well aware of this.

An enlightening study was done in 2015: 200 students participated in a virtual court case simulation. They were presented with

photos of evidence,

 witness accounts,

 and attorney arguments.

The students then discussed the case with 4 jury members: 3 that were of the same opinion as them, and 1 who disagreed.

The jury member who disagreed used an angry tone, with excessive capitalization and exclamation.

In reality, the views were not being expressed by actual people, the responses were pre-programmed and displayed by the computer.

For each student, the angry jury member replied in the same way, with the same capitalized letters and exclamation points. Only...

in half of the cases, he was called Jason...

and in the other half, Alicia.

At the end of the experiment, the angry Jason changed the minds of 18% of the students . . .

And Alicia, **zero**.

What's more, Alicia's angry tone tended to reinforce the students' original opinion.

If a person makes me uncomfortable, I allow myself to make them feel uncomfortable too.

Without raising my voice, without getting angry, but without giving in all the same.

It can just be a case of not laughing at a joke, or politely letting them know that I find their behavior unpleasant.

Oh, new glasses? Very "sexy secretary"!

I stopped just smiling politely.

And all of a sudden, he's the one looking embarrassed.

Nope, just normal glasses, not even new.

At work or in the context of my activism, men are often getting angry at me. And I know that if I react in the same way, I'll be called hysterical.

So I calmly express my irritation.

Quite often, this lowers the tone of the discussion (but it doesn't always work).

And I allow myself to put an end to unpleasant situations.

Even though it's not always easy to do, in the end I think it's the best way to get your message across. The only problem is that it works only if everyone does it.

In any case, those techniques can help in the short term.

But in the long term, we need to teach our children, regardless of their gender,

that anger is a positive emotion, a useful signal.

All the while providing them with the tools to express it in an effective way.

And the next time that you think a woman is being aggressive . . .

. . . you can ask yourself whether you'd think the same thing if it were a man.

It's always good to try to adopt another point of view!

It's January 2017 and my blog has been up for almost a year. I decide to talk about one of the experiences that led me toward feminism: motherhood.

12
The Holidays

Five years ago, I went back to work
at the end of my maternity leave.

At lunch, my colleagues started talking
about their plans for the summer holidays.

I'm off to see my
parents in 2 weeks,
can't wait!

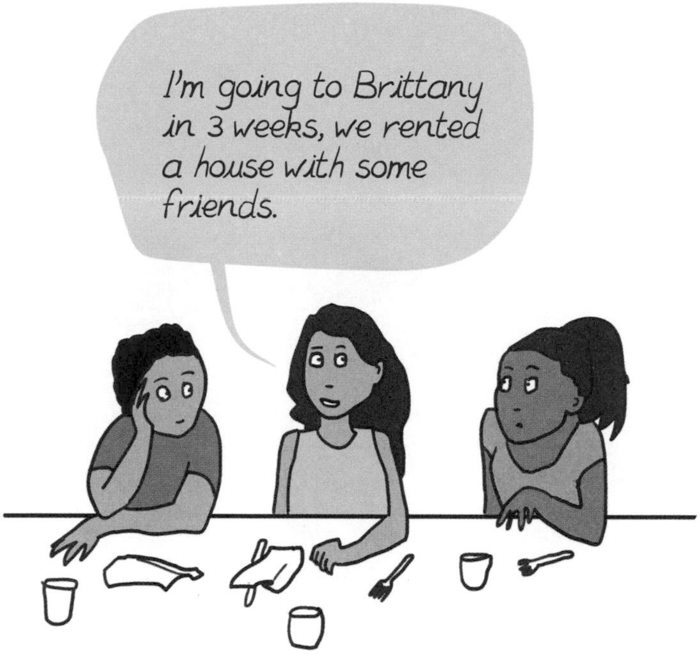
I'm going to Brittany in 3 weeks, we rented a house with some friends.

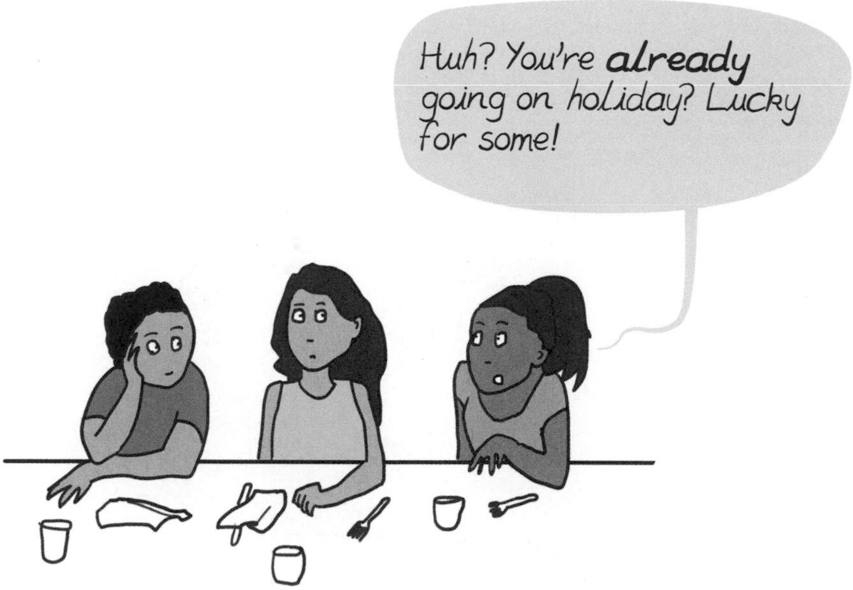
Huh? You're **already** going on holiday? Lucky for some!

I immediately thought back to my childbirth experience.

I was lucky, it was all very quick: just 6 hours of contractions . . .

. . . and 20 minutes of pushing.

I found myself in a room with
my brand-new baby boy.

My old body had clearly packed off to the
Maldives. In its place, I had an empty pouch
instead of a belly, a big bruise where I had the
epidural, and stitches in my pussy.

And just to make me feel even more sexy, I was
decked out with a delightful pair of net panties
complete with giant pads to soak up the blood that
was still oozing out of me.

At 8 p.m. I put my son in his bassinet and closed my eyes.

At 9 p.m. he began crying for a full hour.

At 11 p.m. a pediatric nurse came in.

The crying and the staff's comings and goings were nonstop until the morning. Then a new nurse came into the room.

I hadn't slept, I couldn't understand anything, and I hurt everywhere.

I spent three sleepless nights in the maternity ward. After that, they needed the room, so we took the baby back home.

He was still crying a lot.

At night he had to be fed every three hours.

Each time I had trouble getting him back to sleep. Then I had trouble getting MYSELF back to sleep.

After 11 days, my partner went back to work.

I spent my days alone with a crying baby. In the evening, each minute seemed like an eternity.

Everyone had lots of theories about how I should be handling it.

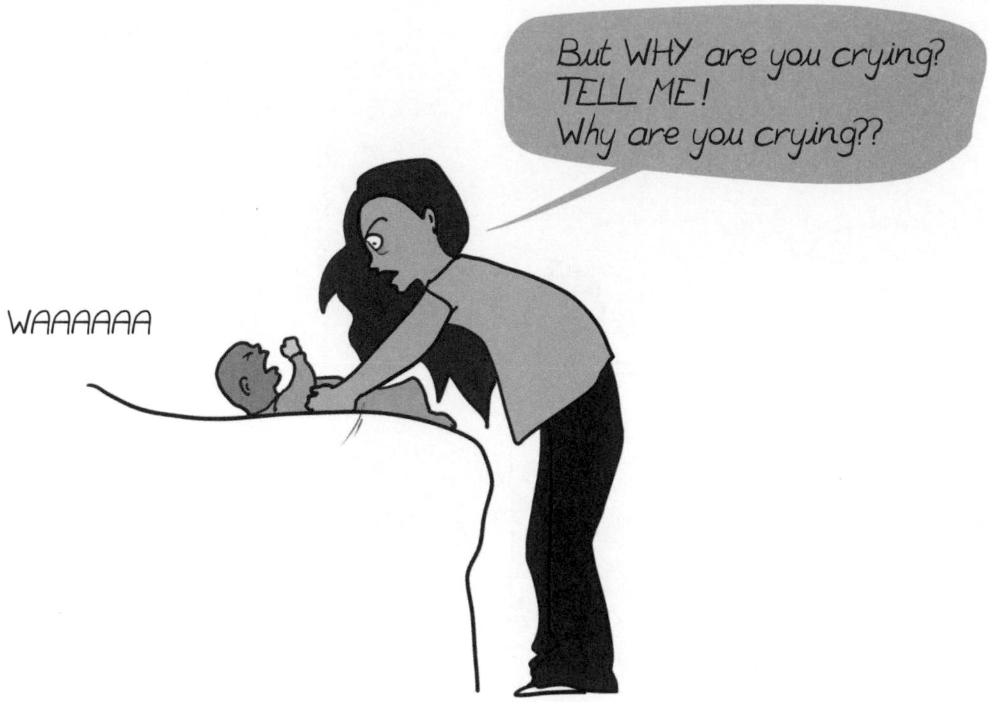
But WHY are you crying?
TELL ME!
Why are you crying??
WAAAAAA

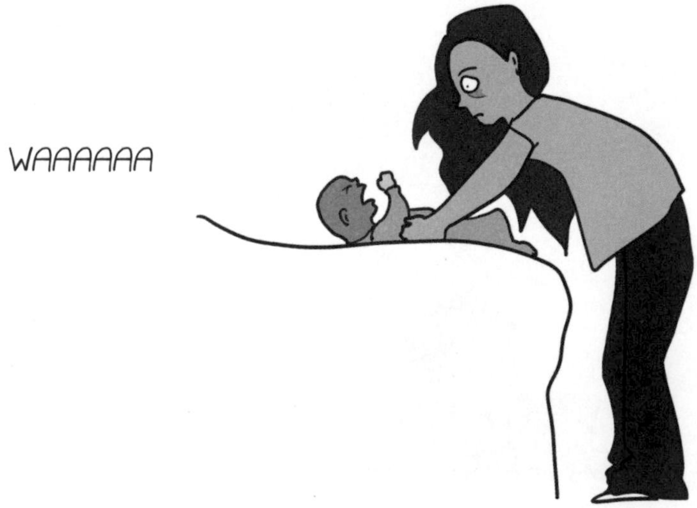
WAAAAAA

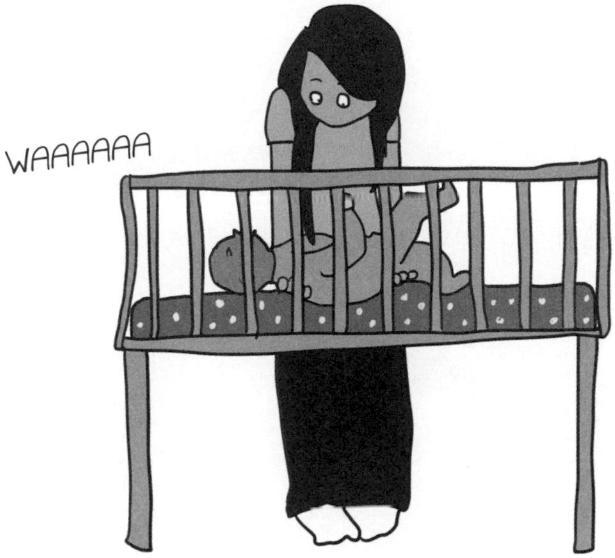
WAAAAAA

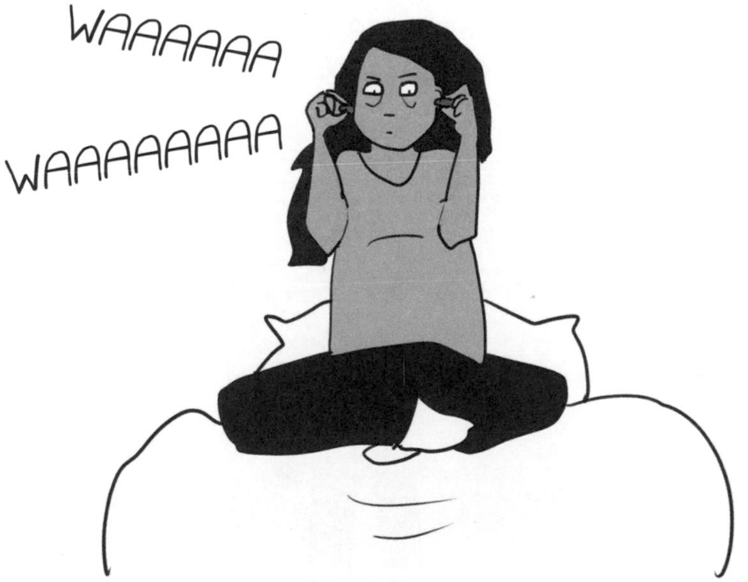
WAAAAAA
WAAAAAAAA

That day, for the first time, I slept for more than an hour.

5 weeks later, my son started to sleep through the night. And that's when I went back to work.

You can do it, strength and honor.

So there you have it, if ever the intention to say "holidays" instead of "maternity leave" crosses your mind, I suggest you think about it twice . . .

Why did she walk off?

I don't know, I didn't say anything . . .

Now, when I hear people talk about postpartum depression and "hormones," it makes me chuckle.

Take any human being, make them go through an ordeal as long, physically challenging, and painful as childbirth, then put them in a small room with an alarm clock that goes off every three hours.

Personally, I call that torture.

But it's very practical to blame a young mom's depression on hormones. It turns her state into something "normal" with a scientific explanation.

But if it wasn't just "hormones," maybe we could . . .

. . . make sure that there was enough space and staff available at night to look after the babies of exhausted mothers . . .

. . . allow the other parent to sleep there too . . .

. . . and provide longer paternity leave . . .

But hey, all of that would require more cash and effort!

It's far more practical to make people believe that there's a universal and innate maternal instinct!

After all, a mom is free!

That's the case in France at least, since in some other countries they decided that it wasn't up to us to do all the work.

Elsewhere, parents can share a partially compensated parental leave.

Sweden: 480 days with 80% compensation

Germany: 367 days with 66% compensation

Italy: 10 months with 30% compensation

...wait for it...

France: 6 months per parent with a "compensation" of €390.52

Also, in Sweden, maternity wards provide a bed for the other parent.

And in Germany, a midwife comes for daily home visits for the first 12 days!

Basically, we can really do better.

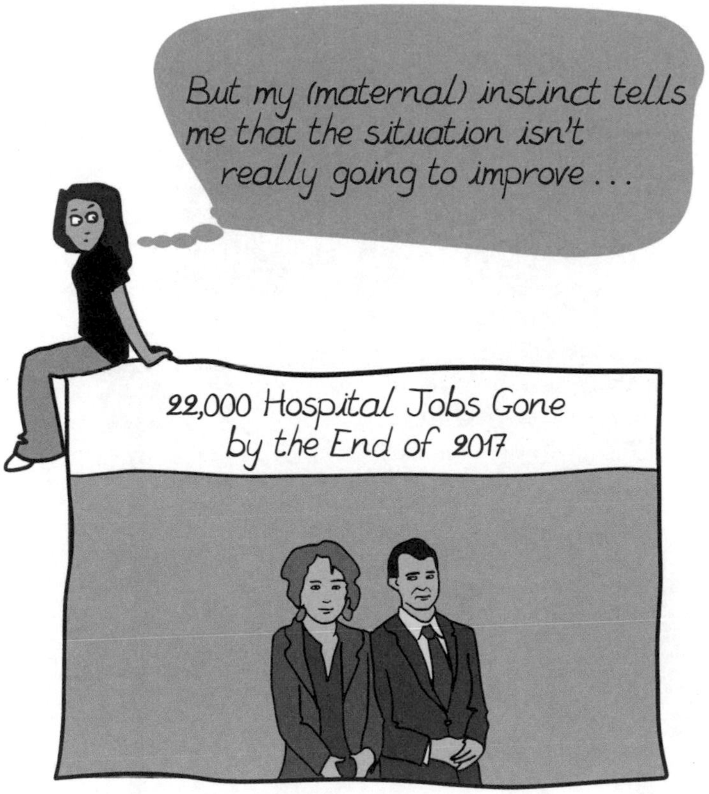
But my (maternal) instinct tells me that the situation isn't really going to improve . . .
22,000 Hospital Jobs Gone by the End of 2017

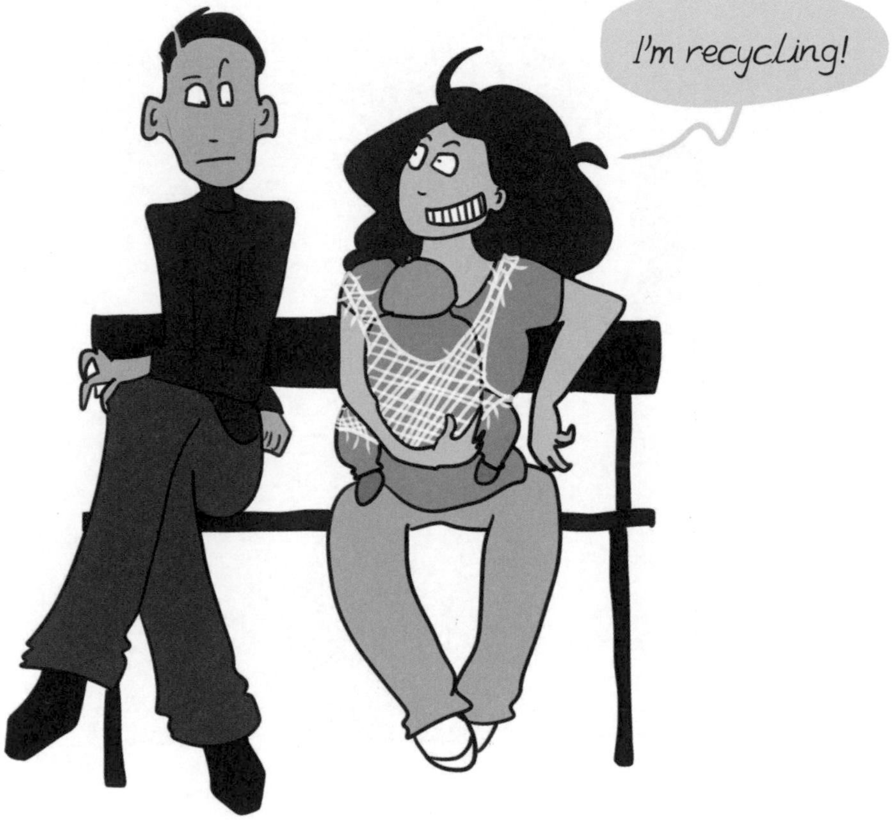
I'm recycling!

A big thank you to my hairy man for
his critical and unconditional support,
to Mom and Dad for having raised
me off the beaten track, and to all
the people who, in one way or another,
contributed to my political awakening.

207

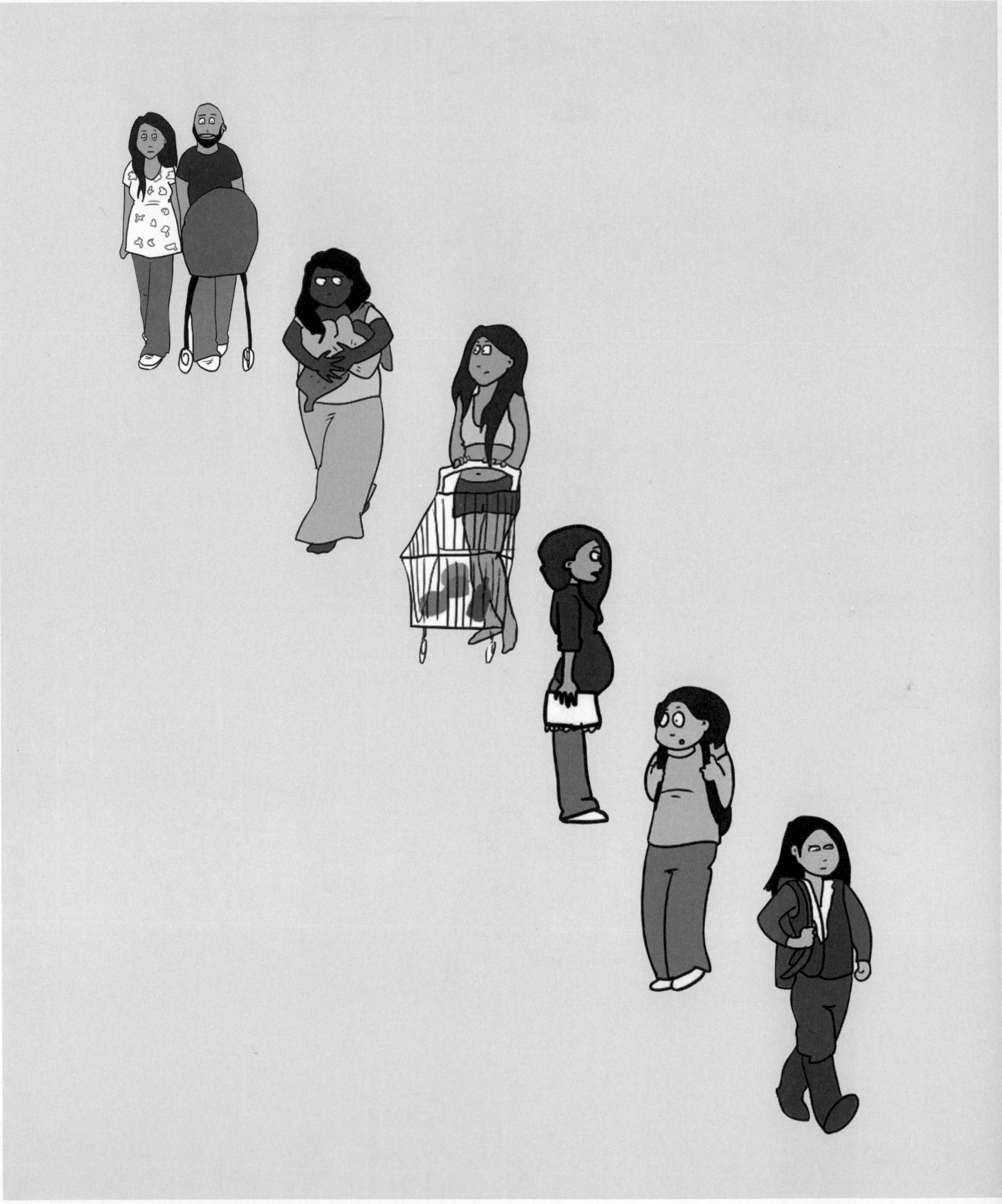